I Look Like My Mother

by Julie K. Lundgren

Science Content Editor:
Shirley Duke

Rourke
Educational Media

rourkeeducationalmedia.com

Teacher Notes available at
rem4teachers.com

Science Content Editor: Shirley Duke holds a bachelor's degree in biology and a master's degree in education from Austin College in Sherman, Texas. She taught science in Texas at all levels for twenty-five years before starting to write for children. Her science books include *You Can't Wear These Genes, Infections, Infestations, and Diseases, Enterprise STEM, Forces and Motion at Work, Environmental Disasters,* and *Gases.* She continues writing science books and also works as a science content editor.

www.rourkeeducationalmedia.com

Photo credits: Cover © Khoroshunova Olga, stefbennett, John L. Absher Pages 2/3 © mathagraphics; Pages 4/5 © Monkey Business Images; Pages 6/7 © Zuzule; Pages 8/9 © David Huntley, RN3dARTS, mathagraphics, Goodluz; Pages 10/11 © Darren J. Bradley; Pages 12/13 © Victor Tyakht, Richard Upshur; Pages 14/15 © Andreas Gradin, Wild At Art; Pages 16/17 © mexrix, Feng Yu; Pages 18/19 © Stefanie van der Vinden, mlorenz , Steven Blandin; Pages 20/21 © olly, Voronin76, Piotr Marcinski, Monkey Business Images

Editor: Kelli Hicks

My Science Library series produced by Blue Door Publishing, Florida for Rourke Educational Media.

Library of Congress PCN Data

Lundgren, Julie K.
I Look Like My Mother / Julie K. Lundgren.
   p. cm. -- (My Science Library)
ISBN 978-1-61810-100-6 (Hard cover) (alk. paper)
ISBN 978-1-61810-233-1 (Soft cover)
Library of Congress Control Number: 2012930300

Rourke Educational Media
Printed in the United States of America,
North Mankato, Minnesota

rourkeeducationalmedia.com
customerservice@rourkeeducationalmedia.com
PO Box 643328 Vero Beach, Florida 32964

Table of Contents

Your Inheritance

Already, your parents have given you an inheritance. What color are your eyes? What color is your hair? Is it curly or straight? Your body's **inherited** characteristics, or traits, come from your parents. The passing of traits from parents to children, called **heredity**, helps make you a unique person.

Parents and children have traits in common.

You inherit more than looks. You can also inherit a food **allergy** or get your first tooth at the same age as one of your parents got their first tooth. Children of parents with peanut allergies, for example, are more likely to have a peanut allergy.

Young animals, including American Paint foals, inherit genes from both their parents.

Plants and animals pass on traits to their offspring, too. Offspring may look similar, but not exactly the same as their parents. The study of heredity is called genetics.

Each parent has two of every **gene**. For many traits, one gene in the pair masks, or **dominates**, the other gene. Offspring inherit one of each gene from their mother and one of each from their father.

If one or both copies of the gene are dominant, the offspring look like the parents. If both copies are the parents' masked gene, then the hidden gene shows and the trait is different than both parents. This explains why some foals of American paint horses can have patterns of spots like their parents, or have no spots at all. Copies of genes that give a foal spots are dominant and copies that make a foal have a solid color are masked in the Paint parents.

Green Thumb Gregor

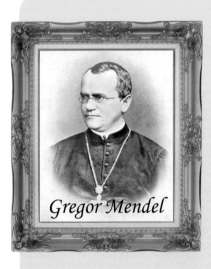

Gregor Mendel

Scientists call Gregor Mendel the father of modern genetics. As a monk in the 1800s in Europe, he grew thousands of pea plants to study how traits, like flower color and seed shape, are passed on from parent plant to offspring. He found that inherited units, now called genes, do not blend but pass from parent to offspring in predictable patterns.

Where Are Your Genes?

The human body contains trillions of cells.

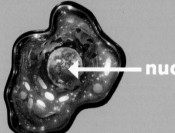

nucleus

Each cell contains a nucleus.

chromosome

Each nucleus contains **chromosomes**. Chromosomes are formed of tightly coiled DNA.

DNA

Each section of DNA contains the genes.

The Next in Line

Living things reproduce as part of their life cycle. Living things pass on traits as a part of reproduction. Each person inherits one set of genes, or instructions, from each parent.

Unlike Gregor Mendel's peas, human traits are often controlled by more than one gene. This makes studying human genetics difficult. A single gene causes our blood type and some diseases, like certain cancers. Scientists study parents and children to learn more about the genetics of the disease and to find the gene that causes the disease. If they can find the gene and understand what is going wrong, they may be able to prevent or cure the disease.

Our bodies follow the instructions written in our genes to form the shape of our fingers, our blood type, and the color of our skin, hair, and eyes.

Male and female sea stars can make offspring together, or a single parent can clone itself. An individual can split through its central disk. For a few months, the two halves will have some small, new growing arms and the fully grown arms from the original adult.

Some plants and animals reproduce by making clones. A clone is an exact copy of its lone parent, with all traits the same.

For some living things, like sea stars and strawberries, reproduction by cloning is normal. Recently, through great expense and time, scientists have found ways to clone large animals like pigs and sheep. Although this cloning is possible, the clones made by scientists often live shorter, less healthy lives. Dolly, the first sheep clone, lived half as long as regular sheep.

Many people debate whether animal cloning is right or wrong and believe it may lead to human cloning. Researchers expect a certain number of failed experiments before making a successful clone. If these failures involved developing human babies, would that be acceptable? What if mistakes only appeared when the human clone reached adulthood? Should researchers clone animals and humans to learn more about the science of genes and cloning? How do you feel about animal and human cloning?

Dolly, The Most Famous Sheep

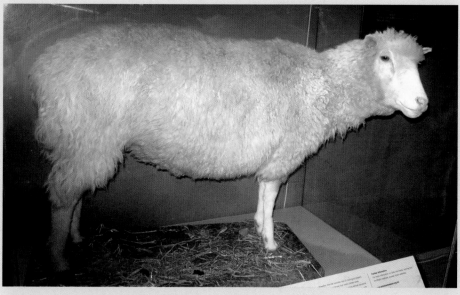

Dolly, born in 1996, suffered from lung cancer at her death just six years later.

Inherited or Learned?

A plant or animal's environment can affect some inherited traits. You may have inherited the trait for tall height, but if you do not have good food to eat in proper amounts, you may not grow tall.

Think about this: genes provide an individual with traits that worked for previous generations. The ability to think and respond to the environment helps an individual survive in its lifetime.

A bird's body has all it needs to produce notes, but it must hear and learn the right songs from its parents in order to communicate with its own kind. Without knowing the songs, the notes mean nothing.

Identical twins share all the same traits. Scientists have studied sets of twins who were separated early in life, often at birth. They were especially interested in comparing pairs of twins where one twin had everything he or she needed and the other twin was deprived of these things. They found that this difference had a big effect on their looks and health in later years.

Learning, too, shapes each of us. We learn the language we speak. We do not inherit it. You may not play soccer well at first, but with practice you can improve. Both learned and inherited traits contribute to who we are.

Practice skills to get better at them.

Grizzly bear mothers teach their young how to fish.

People sometimes argue whether a trait is more influenced by genes, or nature, or more influenced by learning. Is natural ability or talent more important than practice? Is anyone a born leader, or do they learn to be a wise and good leader?

Unfair Treatment: A Seed Planting Experiment

Explore the idea of unfair treatment by experimenting with pea plants. We know plants need good soil, water, and sunlight to grow. What happens if we deny a seed or plant one of these things?

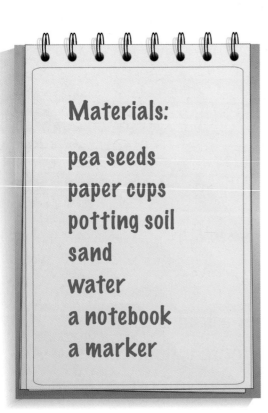

Materials:

pea seeds
paper cups
potting soil
sand
water
a notebook
a marker

Plan Your Experiment

First, you will want to know how a seed grows if it gets everything it needs. This is the **positive control**. Second, you will want to know how a seed grows if it gets none of the things it needs. This is the **negative control**. Then you can plant the experimental cups, one for each thing you want to take away. You will be able to compare the experimental cups to the controls to see if they grow differently.

Label each cup. Place soil or sand in the cups according to the plan.

Plant a seed in each cup. Each day take care of your cups according to your plan. Make daily **observations** and record them in your notebook. How long does it take for the seeds to sprout? How much do they grow each day? Do you see a difference when you compare the experimental cups to the controls?

Successful Living Things

⦿⦿⦿⦿⦿⦿⦿⦿⦿⦿⦿⦿⦿⦿⦿⦿⦿⦿⦿⦿⦿⦿⦿⦿⦿⦿

Many inherited traits help living things have longer, better lives. For example, alert deer that run fast escape predators more easily and more often than slow, unaware deer. Animals who are better adapted for their environment survive.

Swift runners escape hunters and live to reproduce and pass on their genes for speed.

impalas

Po'ouli

Charles Darwin developed this idea of the survival of the fittest in the 1860s as a way to explain how certain traits changed over time in a population of animals or plants. He called it natural selection. For example, the more than 50 kinds of honeycreepers on the island of Hawaii all came from a single kind of bird. These birds developed adaptations over time that allowed them to use different food sources more effectively. Some have long, curved beaks for feeding on the nectar of certain flowers. Others have thick, strong beaks for cracking seeds, and still others have developed thin, short beaks for snapping up insects.

green honeycreeper **purple honeycreeper**

Honeycreepers in other parts of the world have great variety, too. These birds live in tropical areas of South and Central America.

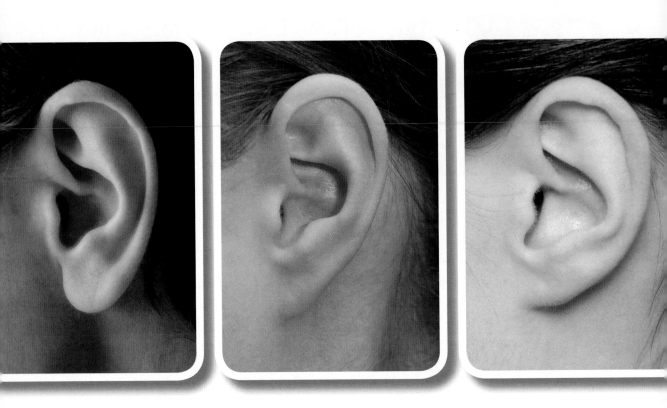

Does earlobe shape affect your survival? Probably not. Can you think of ways it might have at some point in human history?

Other traits do not seem as important for survival. Look in the mirror at your earlobes. What shape are they? Do the lowest points of your ears join directly with your head or do they curve up first? Earlobe shape is inherited. Earlobe shape will not affect your life. It does add to who you are. All of our traits together make each of us a unique and special person.

Researchers have come to understand that our genes and environmental factors both contribute to our looks, behavior, and health. Knowledge about genes that contribute to human diseases like cancer allow doctors to help people who carry these disease genes. Healthy lifestyle choices can often help prevent or slow the appearance of the disease and regular doctor visits allows early disease detection and treatment. By learning about our genetic inheritance, we can make good choices that affect our health today and in the future.

Show What You Know

1. What are some examples of inherited traits?

2. Describe some personal characteristics that are learned.

3. Can you think of inherited traits that *do not seem important* for survival?

Glossary

allergy (AL-er-jee): the body's reaction to something to which it has become very sensitive, like certain foods, insect bites, dust, or pollen

chromosomes (KROH-muh-sohmz): in each living cell, the parts that contain an individual's DNA and genes

dominates (DOM-uh-naytes): in genetics, controls or has the power to mask

gene (JEEN): part of the DNA in the nucleus of a cell of every living thing that determines how you look and the way you grow

heredity (huh-RED-uh-tee): the passing of inherited traits from parents to offspring

inherited (in-HAIR-uh-ted): received characteristics passed on from parent to offspring

negative control (NEG-uh-tiv kuhn-TROHL): in an experiment or test, the trial set that will always give a negative result

observations (ob-zer-VAY-shunz): information from closely watching or examining

positive control (PAHZ-uh-tiv kuhn-TROHL): in an experiment or test, the trial set that will always give a positive result

Index

Websites to Visit

http://kidshealth.org/kid/talk/qa/what_is_gene.html
www.pbs.org/wgbh/nova/genome/heredity.html
www.realtrees4kids.org/ninetwelve/genes.htm

About the Author

Julie K. Lundgren has written more than 40 nonfiction books for children. She gets a kick out of sharing juicy facts about science, nature, and animals, especially if they are slightly disgusting! Through her work, she hopes kids will learn that Earth is an amazing place and young people can make a big difference in keeping our planet healthy. She lives in Minnesota with her family.

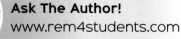
Ask The Author!
www.rem4students.com